The Gondoliers

The Gondoliers

W.S. Gilbert and Arthur Sullivan

MINT EDITIONS

The Gondoliers was first published in 1899.

This edition published by Mint Editions 2021.

ISBN 9781513281476 | E-ISBN 9781513286495

Published by Mint Editions®

MINT
EDITIONS

minteditionbooks.com

Publishing Director: Jennifer Newens
Design & Production: Rachel Lopez Metzger
Project Manager: Micaela Clark
Typesetting: Westchester Publishing Services

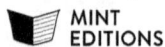

Dramatis Personæ

The Duke of Plaza-Toro (*a Grandee of Spain*)
Luiz (*his Attendant*)
Don Alhambra del Bolero (*the Grand Inquisitor*)
Marco Palmieri
Giuseppe Palmieri
Antonio
Francesco } (*Venetian Gondoliers*)
Giorgio
Annibale
The Duchess of Plaza-Toro
Casilda (*her Daughter*)
Gianetta
Tessa
Fiametta } (*Contadine*)
Vittoria
Giulia
Inez (the King's Foster-mother)

Chorus of Gondoliers and Contadine, Men-at-Arms, Heralds, and Pages.

Act I.—The Piazzetta, Venice.
Act II.—Pavilion in the Palace of Barataria.

(An interval of three months is supposed to elapse
between Acts I and II.)

Date—1750.

Act I

SCENE.—*The Piazzetta, Venice. The Ducal Palace on the right.* FIAMETTA, GIULIA, VITTORIA, *and other Contadine discovered, each tying a bouquet of roses.*

CHORUS OF CONTADINE.

List and learn, ye dainty roses,
    Roses white and roses red,
Why we bind you into posies
    Ere your morning bloom has fled.
By a law of maiden's making,
Accents of a heart that's aching,
Even though that heart be breaking,
    Should by maiden be unsaid:
Though they love with love exceeding,
They must seem to be unheeding—
Go ye then and do their pleading,
    Roses white and roses red!

FIAMETTA.

Two there are for whom, in duty,
    Every maid in Venice sighs—
Two so peerless in their beauty
    That they shame the summer skies.
We have hearts for them, in plenty,
    They have hearts, but all too few,
We, alas, are four-and-twenty!
    They, alas, are only two!
  We, alas!
CHORUS: Alas!
FIA.: Are four-and-twenty,
  They, alas!
CHORUS: Alas!
FIA.: Are only two.
CHORUS: They, alas, are only two, alas!
    Now ye know, ye dainty roses,

Roses white and roses red,
Why we bind you into posies,
Ere your morning bloom has fled,
Roses white and roses red!

(*During this chorus* Antonio, Francesco, Giorgio, *and other Gondoliers have entered unobserved by the Girls—at first two, then two more, then four, then half a dozen, then the remainder of the Chorus*)

Soli.

Franc.: Good morrow, pretty maids; for whom prepare ye
These floral tributes extraordinary?

Fia.: For Marco and Giuseppe Palmieri,
The pink and flower of all the Gondolieri.

Giulia: They're coming here, as we have heard but lately,
To choose two brides from us who sit sedately.

Ant.: Do all you maidens love them?

All: Passionately!

Ant.: These gondoliers are to be envied greatly!

Gior.: But what of us, who one and adore you?
Have pity on our passion, we implore you!

Fia.: These gentlemen must make their choice before you;

Vit.: In the meantime we tacitly ignore you.

Giulia: When they have chosen two that leaves you plenty—
Two dozen we, and, ye are four-and-twenty.

Fia. *and* Vit.: Till then, enjoy your *dolce far niente*.

Ant.: With pleasure, nobody *contradicente*!

Song—Antonio *and* Chorus.

For the merriest fellows are we, tra la,
That ply on the emerald sea, tra la;
With loving and laughing,
And quipping and quaffing,
We're happy as happy can be, tra la—
With loving and laughing, etc.

With sorrow we've nothing to do, tra la,
And care is a thing to pooh-pooh, tra la;

And Jealousy yellow,
Unfortunate fellow,
We drown in the shimmering blue, tra la—
And Jealousy yellow, etc.

FIA. (*looking off*): See, see, at last they come to make their choice—
Let us acclaim them with united voice.

(MARCO *and* GIUSEPPE *appear in gondola at back*)

CHORUS (*Girls*): Hail, hail! gallant gondolieri, ben' venuti! ben' venuti!
Accept our love; our homage, and our duty.
Ben' venuti! ben' venuti!

(MARCO *and* GIUSEPPE *jump ashore—the Girls salute them*)

DUET—MARCO *and* GIUSEPPE, *with* CHORUS OF GIRLS.

MAR. and GIU.: Buon' giorno, signorine!
GIRLS: Gondolieri carissimi!
Siamo contadine!
MAR. and GIU. (*bowing*): Servitors umilissimi!
Per chi questi fiori—
Quests fiori bellissimi?
GIRLS: Per voi, bei signori,
O eccellentissimi!

(*The Girls present their bouquets to* MARCO *and* GIUSEPPE, *who are overwhelmed with them, and carry them with difficulty*)

MAR. and GIU. (*their arms full of flowers*): O ciel'! O ciel'!
GIRLS: Buon' giorno, cavalieri!
MAR. and GIU. (*deprecatingly*): Siamo gondolieri.
(*To* FIA. *and* VIT.). Signorina, io t'amo!
GIRLS (*deprecatingly*): Contadine siamo.
MAR. and GIU.: Signorine!
GIRLS (*deprecatingly*): Contadine!
(*Curtseying to* MAR. *and* GIU.). Cavalieri
MAR. and GIU. (*deprecatingly*): Gondolieri!
Poveri gondolieri!
CHORUS: Buon' giorno, signorine, etc.

DUET—MARCO *and* GIUSEPPE.

We're called *gondolieri*,
But that's a vagary,

It's quite honorary
    The trade that we ply.
For gallantry noted
Since we were short-coated,
To beauty devoted,
    Giuseppe ⎫
    Are Marco ⎭ and I;
When morning is breaking,
Our couches forsaking,
To greet their awaking
    With carols we come.
At summer day's nooning,
When weary lagooning,
Our mandolins tuning,
    We lazily thrum.
When vespers are ringing,
To hope ever clinging,
With songs of our singing
    A vigil we keep,
When daylight is fading,
Enwrapt in night's shading,
With soft serenading
    We sing them to sleep.
We're called *gondolieri*, etc.

RECITATIVE—MARCO *and* GIUSEPPE.

MAR.: And now to choose our brides!
GIU.: As all are young and fair,
    And amiable besides,
BOTH: We really do not care
    A preference to declare.
MAR.: A bias to disclose
    Would be indelicate—
GIU.: And therefore we propose
    To let impartial Fate
    Select for us a mate!
ALL: Viva!
GIRLS: A bias to disclose.

Would be indelicate—

MEN: But how do they propose

    To let impartial Fate

    Select for them a mate?

GIU.: These handkerchiefs upon our eyes be good enough to bind,

MAR.: And take good care that both of us are absolutely blind;

BOTH: Then turn us round—and we, with all convenient despatch,

    Will undertake to marry any two of you we catch!

ALL: Viva!

They undertake to marry any two of $\Big\}$ us they catch!
them they catch!

(*The Girls prepare to bind their eyes as directed*)

FIA. (*to* MARCO): Are you peeping?

    Can you see me?

MAR.: Dark I'm keeping,

    Dark and dreamy! (MARCO *slyly lifts bandage*)

VIT. (*to* GIUSEPPE): If you're blinded

    Truly, say so.

GIU.: All right-minded

    Players play so! (*slyly lifts bandage*).

FIA. (*detecting* MARCO): Conduct shady!

    They are cheating!

    Surely they de-

        Serve a beating! (*replaces bandage*).

VIT. (*detecting* GIUSEPPE): This too much is;

        Maidens mocking—

    Conduct such is

        Truly shocking! (*replaces bandage*).

GIRLS: You can spy, sir!

        Shut your eye, sir!

    You may use it by and by, sir!

ALL: You can see, sir!

        Don't tell me, sir!

    That will do—now let it be, sir!

CHORUS OF GIRLS: My papa he keeps three horses,

        Black, and white, and dapple grey, sir;

    Turn three times, then take your courses,

        Catch whichever girl you may, sir!

CHORUS OF MEN: My papa, etc.

(MARCO *and* GIUSEPPE *turn round, as directed, and try to catch the girls. Business of blind-man's buff. Eventually* MARCO *catches* GIANETTA, *and* GIUSEPPE *catches* TESSA. *The two girls try to escape, but in vain. The two men pass their hands over the girls' faces to discover their identity*)

GIU.: I've at length achieved a capture!

(*Guessing*) This is Tessa! (*removes bandage*). Rapture, rapture!

CHORUS: Rapture, rapture!

MAR. (*guessing*): To me Gianetta fate has granted! (*removes bandage*).

Just the very girl I wanted!

CHORUS: Just the very girl he wanted!

GIU. (*politely to* MAR.): If you'd rather change—

TESS.: My goodness!

This indeed is simple rudeness.

MAR. (*politely to* GIU.): I've no preference whatever

GIA.: Listen to him! Well, I never!

(*Each man kisses each girl*)

GIA.: Thank you, gallant gondolieri!
In a set and formal measure
It is scarcely necessary
To express our pleasure.
Each of us to prove a treasure,
Conjugal and monetary,
Gladly will devote our leisure,
Gallant gondolieri.
Tra, la, la, la, la, la, etc.

TESS.: Gay and gallant *gondolieri*,
Take us both and hold us tightly,
You have luck extraordinary;
We might have been unsightly!
If we judge your conduct rightly,
'Twas a choice involuntary;
Still we thank you most politely,
Gay and gallant gondolieri!—
Tra, la, la, la, la, la, etc.

CHORUS OF GIRLS: Thank you, gallant gondolieri;
In a set and formal measure,
It is scarcely necessary
To express our pleasure.
Each of us to prove a treasure

Gladly will devote our leisure,
Gay and gallant *gondolieri*!
Tra, la, la, la, la, la, etc.
ALL: Fate in this has put his finger
Let us bow to Fate's decree,
Then no longer let us linger,
To the altar hurry we!

(*They all dance off two and two* GIANETTA *with* MARCO, TESSA *with* GIUSEPPE)

(*Flourish. A gondola arrives at the Piazzetta steps, from which enter the* DUKE OF PLAZA-TORO, *the* DUCHESS, *their daughter* CASILDA, *and their attendant* LUIZ, *who carries a drum. All are dressed in pompous but old and faded clothes*)

(*Entrance of* DUKE, DUCHESS, CASILDA, *and* LUIZ)

DUKE: From the sunny Spanish shore,
The Duke of Plaza-Tor'—
DUCH.: And His Grace's Duchess true—
CAS.: And His Grace's daughter, too—
LUIZ: And His Grace's private drum
To Venetia's shores have come:
ALL: If ever, ever, ever
They get back to Spain,
They will never, never, never
Cross the sea again—
DUKE: Neither that Grandee from the Spanish shore,
The noble Duke of Plaza Tor'—
DUCH.: Nor His Grace's Duchess, staunch and true—
CAS.: You may add, His Grace's daughter, too—
LUIZ: Nor His Grace's own particular drum
To Venetia's shores will come:
ALL: If ever, ever, ever
They get back to Spain,
They will never, never, never
Cross the sea again!

DUKE: At last we have arrived at our destination. This is the Ducal Palace, and it is here that the Grand Inquisitor resides. As a Castilian hidalgo of ninety-five quarterings, I regret that I am unable to pay my state visit on a horse. As a Castilian hidalgo of that description, I should have preferred to ride through the streets of Venice; but owing, I presume, to an unusually wet season, the streets are in such a condition that equestrian exercise is impracticable. No matter. Where is our suite?

LUIZ (*coming forward*): Your Grace, I am here.

DUCH.: Why do you not do yourself the honour to kneel when you address His Grace?

DUKE: My love, it is so small a matter! (*To* LUIZ) Still, you may as well do it. (LUIZ *kneels*)

CAS.: The young man seems to entertain but an imperfect appreciation of the respect due from a menial to a Castilian hidalgo.

DUKE: My child, you are hard upon our suite.

CAS.: Papa, I've no patience with the presumption of persons in his plebeian position. If he does not appreciate that position, let him be whipped until he does.

DUKE: Let us hope the omission was not intended as a slight. I should be much hurt if I thought it was. So would he. (*To* LUIZ.) Where are the halberdiers who were to have had the honour of meeting us here, that our visit to the Grand Inquisitor might be made in becoming state?

LUIZ: Your Grace, the halberdiers are mercenary people who stipulated for a trifle on account.

DUKE: How tiresome! Well, let us hope the Grand Inquisitor is a blind gentleman. And the band who were to have had the honour of escorting us? I see no band!

LUIZ: Your Grace, the band are sordid persons who required to be paid in advance.

DUCH.: That's so like a band!

DUKE (*annoyed*): Insuperable difficulties meet me at every turn!

DUCH.: But surely they know His Grace?

LUIZ: Exactly—they know His Grace.

DUKE: Well, let us hope that the Grand Inquisitor is a deaf gentleman, a cornet-à-piston would be something. You do not happen to possess the accomplishment of tootling like a cornet-à-piston?

LUIZ: Alas, no, Your Grace! But I can imitate a farmyard.

DUKE (*doubtfully*): I don't see how that would help us. I don't see how we could bring it in.

CAS.: It would not help us in the least. We are not a parcel of graziers come to market, dolt! (LUIZ *rises*)

DUKE: My love, our suite's feelings! (*To* LUIZ.) Be so good as to ring the bell and inform the Grand Inquisitor that his Grace the Duke of Plaza-Toro, Count Matadoro, Baron Picadoro—

DUCH.: And suite—

DUKE: And suite—have arrived at Venice, and seek—

CAS.: Desire—

DUCH.: Demand!

DUKE: And demand an audience.

LUIZ: Your Grace has but to command.

DUKE (*much moved*): I felt sure of it—I felt sure of it! (*Exit* LUIZ *into Ducal Palace*) And now, my love—(*Aside to* DUCHESS.) Shall we tell her? I think so—(*Aloud to* CASILDA.) And now, my love, prepare for a magnificent surprise. It is my agreeable duty to reveal to you a secret which should make you the happiest young lady in Venice!

CAS.: A secret?

DUCH.: A secret which, for State reasons, it has been necessary to preserve for twenty years.

DUKE: When you were a prattling babe of six months old you were married by proxy to no less a personage than the infant son and heir of His Majesty the immeasurably wealthy King of Barataria!

CAS.: Married to the infant son of the King of Barataria? Was I consulted? (DUKE *shakes his head*) Then it was a most unpardonable liberty!

DUKE: Consider his extreme youth and forgive him. Shortly after the ceremony that misguided monarch abandoned the creed of his forefathers, and became a Wesleyan Methodist of the most bigoted and persecuting type. The Grand Inquisitor, determined that the innovation should not be perpetuated in Barataria, caused your smiling and unconscious husband to be stolen and conveyed to Venice. A fortnight since the Methodist Monarch and all his Wesleyan Court were killed in an insurrection, and we are here to ascertain the whereabouts of your husband, and to hail you, our daughter, as Her Majesty, the reigning Queen of Barataria! (*Kneels*)

(*During this speech* LUIZ *re-enters*)

DUCH.: Your Majesty! (*Kneels*) (*Drum roll*)

DUKE: It is at such moments as these that one feels how necessary it is to travel with a full band.

CAS.: I, the Queen of Barataria! But I've nothing to wear! We are practically penniless!

DUKE: That point has not escaped me. Although I am unhappily in straitened circumstances at present, my social influence is something enormous; and a Company, to be called the Duke of Plaza-Toro, Limited, is in course of formation to work me. An influential directorate has been secured, and I shall myself join the Board after allotment.

CAS.: Am to understand that the Queen of Barataria may be called upon at any time to witness her honoured sire in process of liquidation?

DUCH.: The speculation is not exempt from that drawback. If your father should stop, it will, of course, be necessary to wind him up.

CAS.: But it's so undignified it's so degrading! A Grandee of Spain turned into a public company! Such a thing was never heard of!

DUKE: My child, the Duke of Plaza-Toro does not follow fashions— he leads them. He always leads everybody. When he was in the army he led his regiment. He occasionally led them into action. He invariably led them out of it.

SONG—DUKE OF PLAZA-TORO.

In enterprise of martial kind,
    When there was any fighting,
He led his regiment from behind—
    He found it less exciting.
But when away his regiment ran,
    His place was at the fore, O—
        That celebrated,
        Cultivated,
        Underrated
          Nobleman,
    The Duke of Plaza-Toro!

ALL: In the first and foremost flight, ha, ha!
    You always found that knight, ha, ha!
        That celebrated,
        Cultivated,
        Underrated
        Nobleman,
    The Duke of Plaza-Toro!

When, to evade Destruction's hand,
    To hide they all proceeded,
No soldier in that gallant band
    Hid half as well as he did.
He lay concealed throughout the war,
    And so preserved his gore, O!
        That unaffected,
        Undetected,
        Well-connected
          Warrior,
    The Duke of Plaza-Toro!
ALL: In every doughty deed, ha, ha!
    He always took the lead, ha, ha!
        That unaffected,
        Undetected,
        Well-connected
          Warrior,
    The Duke of Plaza-Toro!

When told that they would all be shot
    Unless they left the service,
That hero hesitated not,
    So marvellous his nerve is.
He sent his resignation in,
    The first of all his corps, O!
        That very knowing,
        Overflowing,
        Easy-going
          Paladin,
    The Duke of Plaza-Toro!
ALL: To men of grosser clay, -ha, ha!
    He always showed the way, ha, ha!
        That very knowing,
        Overflowing,
        Easy-going
          Paladin,
    The Duke of Plaza-Toro!

(*Exeunt* DUKE *and* DUCHESS *into Ducal Palace. As soon as they have disappeared,* LUIZ *and* CASILDA *rush to each other's arms*)

Recitative and Duet—Casilda *and* Luiz.

BOTH: O rapture, when alone together
    Two loving hearts and those that bear them
  May join in temporary tether,
    Though Fate apart should rudely tear them.
CAS.: Necessity, Invention's mother,
    Compelled me to a course of feigning—
  But, left alone with one another,
    I will atone for my disdaining!

  Ah, well-beloved,
  Mine angry frown
  Is but a gown
  That serves to dress
  My gentleness!
LUIZ: Ah, well-beloved,
  Thy cold disdain It gives no pain—
  'Tis mercy, played
  In masquerade!
BOTH: Ah, well-beloved, etc.

CAS.: O Luiz, Luiz—what have you said? What have I done? What have I allowed you to do?

LUIZ: Nothing, I trust, that you will ever have reason to repent. (*Offering to embrace her*)

CAS. (*withdrawing from him*): Nay, Luiz, it may not be. I have embraced you for the last time.

LUIZ (*amazed*): Casilda!

CAS.: I have just learnt, to my surprise and indignation, that I was wed in babyhood to the infant son of the King of Barataria!

LUIZ: The son of the King of Barataria? The child who was stolen in infancy by the Inquisition?

CAS.: The same. But, of course, you know his story.

LUIZ: Know his story? Why, I have often told you that my mother was the nurse to whose charge he was entrusted!

CAS.: True. I had forgotten. Well, he has been discovered, and my father has brought me here to claim his hand.

LUIZ: But you will not recognize this marriage? It took place when you were too young to understand its import.

CAS.: Nay, Luiz, respect my principles and cease to torture me with vain entreaties. Henceforth my life is another's.

LUIZ: But stay—the present and the future—they are anther's; but the past—that at least is ours, and none can take it from us. As we may revel in naught else, let us revel in that!

CAS.: I don't think I grasp your meaning.

LUIZ: Yet it is logical enough. You say you cease to love me?

CAS. (*demurely*): I say I *may* not love you.

LUIZ: Ah, but you do not say you *did* not love me?

CAS.: I loved you with a frenzy that words are powerless to express—and that but ten brief minutes since!

LUIZ: Exactly. My own—that is, until ten minutes since, my own—my lately loved, my recently adored—tell me that until, say a quarter of an hour ago, I was all in all to thee! (*Embracing her*)

CAS.: I see your idea. It's ingenious, but don't do that. (*Releasing herself*)

LUIZ: There can be no harm in revelling in the past.

CAS.: None whatever, but an embrace cannot be taken to act retrospectively.

LUTZ: Perhaps not! Casilda, you were to me as the sun is to the earth!

CAS.: And now our love, so full of life, is but a silent, solemn memory!

LUIZ: Must it be so, Casilda?

CAS.: Luiz, it must be so!

DUET—CASILDA *and* LUIZ.

LUIZ: There was a time—
  A time for ever gone—ah, woe is me!
 It was no crime
  To love but thee alone—ah, woe is me!
 One heart, one life, one soul,
 One aim, one goal—
  Each in the other's thrall,
  Each all in all, ah, woe is me!
BOTH: Oh, bury, bury—let the grave close o'er
 The days that were—that never will be more!
 Oh, bury, bury love that all condemn,
 And let the whirlwind mourn its requiem!

CAS.: Dead as the last year's leaves—
   As gathered flowers—ah, woe is me!
Dead as the garnered sheaves,
   That love of ours—ah, woe is me!
Born but to fade and die
When hope was high,
   Dead and as far away
   As yesterday!—ah, woe is me!

BOTH: Oh, bury, bury—let the grave close o'er, etc.

(*Re-enter from the Ducal Palace the* DUKE *and* DUCHESS, *followed by* DON ALHAMBRA DEL BOLERO, *the Grand Inquisitor*)

DUKE: My child, allow me to present to you His Distinction Don Alhambra del Bolero, the Grand Inquisitor of Spain. It was His Distinction who so thoughtfully abstracted your infant husband and brought him to Venice.

DON AL.: So this is the little lady who is so unexpectedly called upon to assume the functions of Royalty! And a very nice little lady, too!

DUKE: Jimp, isn't she?

DON AL.: Distinctly jimp. Allow me! (*Offers his hand. She turns away mp. scornfully*) Naughty temper!

DUKE: You must make some allowance. Her Majesty's head is a little turned by her access of dignity.

DON AL.: I could have wished that Her Majesty's access of dignity had turned it in this direction.

DUCH.: Unfortunately, if I am not mistaken, there appears to be some little doubt as to His Majesty's whereabouts.

CAS. (*aside*): A doubt as to his whereabouts? Then we may yet be saved!

DON AL.: A doubt? Oh dear, no—no doubt at all! He is here, in Venice, plying the modest but picturesque calling of a gondolier. I can give you his address—I see him every day! In the entire annals of our history there is absolutely no circumstance so entirely free from all manner of doubt of any kind whatever! Listen, and I'll tell you all about it.

SONG—DON ALHAMBRA (*with* DUKE, DUCHESS, CASILDA, *and* LUIZ).

I stole the Prince, and I brought him here,
   And left him gaily prattling

With a highly respectable gondolier,
Who promised the Royal babe to rear,
And teach him the trade of a timoneer
 With his own beloved bratling.

 Both of the babes were strong and stout,
  And, considering all things, clever.
 Of that there is no manner of doubt—
 No probable, possible shadow of doubt—
  No possible doubt whatever.
ALL: No possible doubt whatever.
 Time sped, and when at the end of a year
  I sought that infant cherished,
That highly respectable gondolier
Was lying a corpse on his humble bier—
I dropped a Grand Inquisitor's tear—
 That gondolier had perished.

 A taste for drink, combined with gout,
  Had doubled him up-for ever.
 Of *that* there is no manner of doubt—
 No probable, possible shadow of doubt—
  No possible doubt whatever.
ALL: No possible doubt whatever.
 But owing, I'm much disposed to fear,
  To his terrible taste for tippling,
That highly respectable gondolier
Could never declare with a mind sincere
Which of the two was his offspring dear,
 And which the Royal stripling!

 Which was which he could never make out
  Despite his best endeavour.
 Of *that* there is no manner of doubt—
 No probable, possible shadow of doubt—
  No possible doubt whatever.
ALL: No possible doubt whatever.
 The children followed his old career—
  (This statement can't be parried)

Of a highly respectable gondolier:
Well, one of the two (who will soon be here)—
But *which* of the two is not quite clear—
   Is the Royal Prince you married!

   Search in and out and round about,
    And you'll discover never
   A tale so free from every doubt—
   All probable, possible shadow of doubt—
    All possible doubt whatever!

ALL: A tale so free from, every doubt, etc.

CAS.: Then do you mean to say that I am married to one of two gondoliers, but it is impossible to say which?

DON AL.: Without any doubt of any kind whatever. But be reassured: the nurse to whom your husband was entrusted is the mother of the musical young man who is such a past-master of that delicately modulated instrument (*Indicating the drum.*). She can, no doubt, establish the King's identity beyond all question.

LUIZ: Heavens, how did he know that?

DON AL.: My young friend, a Grand Inquisitor is always up to date. (*To* CAS.) His mother is at present the wife of a highly respectable and old-established brigand, who carries on an extensive practice in the mountains around Cordova. Accompanied by two of my emissaries, he will set off at once for his mother's address. She will return with them, and if she finds any difficulty in making up her mind, the persuasive influence of the torture chamber will jog her memory.

RECITATIVE—CASILDA *and* DON ALHAMBRA.

CAS.: But, bless my heart, consider my position!
   I am the wife of one, that's very clear;
But who can tell, except by intuition,
   Which is the Prince, and which the Gondolier?

DON AL.: Submit to Fate without unseemly wrangle:
   Such complications frequently occur—
Life is one closely complicated tangle:
   Death is the only true unraveller!

QUINTET—DUKE, DUCHESS, CASILDA, LUIZ, *and*
DON ALHAMBRA.

ALL: Try we life-long, we can never
  Straighten out life's tangled skein,
  Why should we, in vain endeavour,
    Guess and guess and guess again?
LUIZ: Life's a pudding full of plums,
DUCH.: Care's a canker that benumbs.
ALL: Life's a pudding full of plums,
      Care's a canker that benumbs.
  Wherefore waste our elocution
  On impossible solution?
  Life's a pleasant institution,
    Let us take it as it comes!
  Set aside the dull enigma,
    We shall guess it all too soon;
  Failure brings no kind of stigma—
    Dance we to another tune!
      String the lyre and fill the cup,
      Lest on sorrow we should sup.
      String the lyre and fill the cup,
      Lest on sorrow we should sup.
  Hop and skip to Fancy's fiddle,
  Hands across and down the middle—
  Life's perhaps the only riddle
    That we shrink from giving up!
(*Exeunt all into Ducal Palace except* LUIZ, *who goes off in gondola*)
(*Enter Gondoliers and Contadine, followed by* MARCO, GIANETTA,
GIUSEPPE, *and* TESSA)

CHORUS.

  Bridegroom, and bride!
    Knot that's insoluble,
    Voices all voluble
  Hail it with pride.
  Bridegroom and bride!
    We in sincerity

>   Wish you prosperity,
>   Bridegroom and bride!

SONG—TESSA.

TESS.: When a merry maiden marries,
    Sorrow goes and pleasure tarries;
        Every sound becomes a song,
        All is right, and nothing's wrong!
    From to-day and ever after
    Let our tears be tears of laughter.
        Every sigh that finds a vent
        Be a sigh of sweet content!
    When you marry, merry maiden,
    Then the air with love is laden;
        Every flower is a rose,
          Every goose becomes a swan,
        Every kind of trouble goes
          Where the last year's snows have gone!
CHORUS: Sunlight takes the place of shade
    When you marry, merry maid!
TESS.: When a merry maiden marries,
    Sorrow goes and pleasure tarries;
        Every sound becomes a song,
        All is right, and nothing's wrong.
    Gnawing Care and aching Sorrow,
    Get ye gone until to-morrow;
        Jealousies in grim array,
        Ye are things of yesterday!
    When you marry, merry maiden,
    Then the air with joy is laden;
        All the corners of the earth
          Ring with music sweetly played,
        Worry is melodious mirth,
          Grief is joy in masquerade;
CHORUS: Sullen night is laughing day—
    All the year is merry May!
(*At the end of the song,* DON ALHAMBRA *enters at back. The Gondoliers and Contadine shrink from him, and gradually go off, much alarmed*)

GIU.: And now our lives are going to begin in real earnest! What's a bachelor? A mere nothing—he's a chrysalis. He can't be said to live—he exists.

MAR.: What a delightful institution marriage is! Why have we wasted all this time? Why didn't we marry ten years ago?

TESS.: Because you couldn't find anybody nice enough.

GIA.: Because you were waiting for *us*.

MAR.: I suppose that *was* the reason. We were waiting for you without knowing it. (DON ALHAMBRA *comes forward*) Hallo!

DON AL.: Good morning.

GIU.: If this gentleman is an undertaker, it's a bad omen.

DON AL. Ceremony of some sort going on?

GIU. (*aside*): He *is* an undertaker! (*Aloud*) No—a little unimportant family gathering. Nothing in *your* line.

DON AL.: Somebody's birthday, suppose?

GIA.: Yes, mine!

TESS.: And mine!

MAR.: And mine!

GIU.: And mine!

DON AL.: Curious coincidence! And how old may you all be?

TESS.: It's a rude question—but about ten minutes.

DON AL.: Remarkably fine children! But surely you are jesting?

TESS.: In other words, we were married about ten minutes since.

DON AL.: Married! You don't mean to say you are married?

MAR.: Oh yes, we are married.

DON AL.: What, both of you?

ALL: All four of us.

DON AL. (*aside*): Bless my heart, how extremely awkward!

GIA.: You don't mind, I suppose?

TESS.: You were not thinking of either of us for yourself, I presume? Oh, Giuseppe, look at him—he was. He's heart-broken!

DON AL.: No, no, I wasn't! I wasn't!

GIU.: Now, my man (*slapping him on the back*), we don't want anything in your line to-day, and if your curiosity's satisfied— you can go!

DON AL.: You mustn't call me your man. It's a liberty. I don't think you know who I am.

GIU.: Not we, indeed! We are jolly gondoliers, the sons of Baptisto Palmieri, who led the last revolution. Republicans, heart and soul, we hold all men to be equal. As we abhor oppression, we abhor kings: as we detest vain-glory, we detest rank: as we despise effeminacy, we despise wealth. We are Venetian gondoliers—your equals in everything except our calling; and in that at once your masters and your servants.

DON AL.: Bless my heart, how unfortunate! One of you may be Baptisto's son, for anything know to the contrary; but the other is no less a personage than the only son of the late King of Barataria.

ALL: What!

DON AL.: And I trust—I *trust* it was that one who slapped me on the shoulder and called me his man!

GIU.: One of us a king!

MAR.: Not brothers!

TESS.: The King of Barataria!

GIA.: Well, who'd have thought it!

MAR.: But which is it?

(Together)

DON AL.: What does it matter? As you are both Republicans, and hold kings in detestation, of course you'll abdicate at once. Good morning! (*Going*)

GIA. and TESS.: Oh, don't do that! (MARCO *and* GIUSEPPE *stop him*)

GIU.: Well, as to that, of course there are kings and kings. When I say that I detest kings, I mean I detest *bad* kings.

DON AL.: I see. It's a delicate distinction.

GIU.: Quite so. Now I can conceive a kind of king—an ideal king—the creature of my fancy, you know—who would be absolutely unobjectionable. A king, for instance, who would abolish taxes and make everything cheap, except gondolas—

MAR.: And give a great many free entertainments to the gondoliers—

GIU.: And let off fireworks on the Grand Canal, and engage all the gondolas for the occasion—

MAR.: And scramble money on the Rialto among the gondoliers.

GIU.: Such a king would be a blessing to his people, and if I were a king, that is the sort of king I would be.

MAR.: And so would I!

DON AL.: Come, I'm glad to find your objections are not insuperable.

MAR. and GIU.: Oh, they're not insuperable.

GIA. and TESS: No, they're not insuperable.

GIU.: Besides, we are open to conviction.

GIA.: Yes; they are open to conviction.

Tess.: Oh, they've often been convicted.

Giu.: Our views may have been hastily formed on insufficient grounds. They may be crude, ill-digested, erroneous. I've a very poor opinion of the politician who is not open to conviction.

Tess. (*to* Gia.): Oh, he's a fine fellow!

Gia.: Yes, that's the sort of politician for my money!

Don Al.: Then we'll consider it settled. Now, as the country is in a state of insurrection, it is absolutely necessary that you should assume the reins of Government at once; and, until it is ascertained which of you is to be king, I have arranged that you will reign jointly, so that no question can arise hereafter as to the validity of any of your acts.

Mar.: As one individual?

Don Al.: As one individual.

Giu. (*linking himself with* Marco): Like this?

Don Al.: Something like that.

Mar.: And we may take our friends with us, and give them places about the Court?

Don Al.: Undoubtedly. That's always done!

Mar.: I'm convinced!

Giu.: So am I!

Tess.: Then the sooner we're off the better.

Gia.: We'll just run home and pack up a few things (*Going*)—

Don Al.: Stop, stop—that won't do at all—ladies are not admitted.

All: What!

Don Al.: Not admitted. Not at present. Afterwards, perhaps. We'll see.

Giu.: Why, you don't mean to say you are going to separate us from our wives!

Don Al.: (*aside*). This is very awkward! (*Aloud*) Only for a time—a few months. After all, what is a few months?

Tess.: But we've only been married half an hour! (*Weeps*)

Finale, Act I.

Song—Gianetta.

Kind sir, you cannot have the heart
    Our lives to part
   From those to whom an hour ago

We were united!
Before our flowing hopes you stem,
    Ah, look at them,
    And pause before you deal this blow,
       All uninvited!
You men can never understand
    That heart and hand
    Cannot be separated when
       We go a-yearning;
You see, you've only women's eyes
    To idolize
    And only women's hearts, poor men,
       To set *you* burning!
Ah me, you men will never understand
That woman's heart is one with woman's hand!

Some kind of charm you seem to find
    In womankind—
    Some source of unexplained delight
       (Unless you're jesting),
But what attracts you, I confess,
    I cannot guess,
    To me a woman's face is quite
       Uninteresting!
If from my sister I were torn,
    It could be borne—
    I should, no doubt, be horrified,
       But I could bear it;—
But Marco's quite another thing—
    He is my King,
    He has my heart and none beside
       Shall ever share it!
Ah me, you men will never understand
That woman's heart is one with woman's hand!

RECITATIVE—DON ALHAMBRA.

Do not give way to this uncalled-for grief,
Your separation will be very brief.

To ascertain which is the King
  And which the other,
To Barataria's Court I'll bring
  His foster-mother;
Her former nurseling to declare
  She'll be delighted.
That settled, let each happy pair
  Be reunited.

MAR., GIU., GIA., TESS.: Viva! His argument is strong!
 Viva! We'll not be parted long!
 Viva! It will be settled soon!
 Viva! Then comes our honeymoon!

(*Exit* DON ALHAMBRA)

QUARTET—MARCO, GIUSEPPE, GIANETTA, TESSA.

GIA.: Then one of us will be a Queen,
  And sit on a golden throne,
   With a crown instead
   Of a hat on her head,
  And diamonds all her own!
 With a beautiful robe of gold and green,
  I've always understood;
   I wonder whether
   Shed wear a feather?
  I rather think she should!

ALL: Oh, 'tis a glorious thing, I ween,
 To be a regular Royal Queen!
 No half-and-half affair, I mean,
 But a right-down regular Royal Queen!

MAR.: She'll drive about in a carriage and pair,
  With the King on her left-hand side,
   And a milk-white horse,
   As a matter of course,
  Whenever she wants to ride!
 With beautiful silver shoes to wear
  Upon her dainty feet;
   With endless stocks
   Of beautiful frocks

And as much as she wants to eat!
ALL: Oh, 'tis a glorious thing, I ween, etc.
TESS.: Whenever she condescends to walk,
  Be sure she'll shine at that,
   With her haughty stare
   And her nose in the air,
  Like a well-born aristocrat!
 At elegant high society talk
  She'll bear away the bell,
   With her 'How de do?'
   And her 'How are you?'
   And 'I trust I see you well!'
ALL: Oh, 'tis a glorious thing, I ween, etc.
GIU.: And noble lords will scrape and bow,
  And double themselves in two,
   And open their eyes
   In blank surprise
  At whatever she likes to do.
 And everybody will roundly vow
  She's fair as flowers in May,
   And say, 'How clever!'
   At whatsoever
  She condescends to say!
ALL: Oh, 'tis a glorious thing, I ween,
 To be a regular Royal Queen!
 No half-and-half affair, I mean,
 But a right-down regular Royal Queen!
(*Enter Chorus of Gondoliers and Contadine*)

CHORUS.

 Now, pray, what is the cause of this remarkable hilarity?
  This sudden ebullition of unmitigated jollity?
 Has anybody blessed you with a sample of his charity?
  Or have you been adopted by a gentleman of quality?
MAR. and GIU.: Replying, we sing
  As one individual,
 As I find I'm a king,
  To my kingdom I bid you all.

I'm aware you object
    To pavilions and palaces,
But you'll find I respect
    Your Republican fallacies.
CHORUS: As they know we object
    To pavilions and palaces,
How can they respect
    Our Republican fallacies?
MAR.: For every one who feels inclined,
Some post we undertake to find
Congenial with his frame of mind—
    And all shall equal be.
GIU.: The Chancellor in his peruke—
The Earl, the Marquis, and the Dook,
The Groom, the Butler, and the Cook—
    They all shall equal be.
MAR.: The Aristocrat who banks with Coutts—
The Aristocrat who hunts and shoots—
The Aristocrat who cleans our boots
    They all shall equal be!
GIU.: The Noble Lord who rules the State—
The Noble Lord who cleans the plate—
MAR.: The Noble Lord who scrubs the grate.—
    They all shall equal be!
GIU.: The Lord High Bishop orthodox—
The Lord High Coachman on the box—
MAR.: The Lord High Vagabond in the stocks—
    They all shall equal be!
BOTH: For every one, etc.
Sing high, sing low,
Wherever they go,
    They all shall equal be!
CHORUS: Sing high, sing low,
Wherever they go,
    They all shall equal be!

The Earl, the Marquis, and the Dook,
The Groom, the Butler, and the Cook,
The Aristocrat who banks with Coutts,

The Aristocrat who cleans the boots,
The Noble Lord who rules the State,
The Noble Lord who scrubs the grate,
The Lord High Bishop orthodox,
The Lord High Vagabond in the stocks—

For every one, etc.

> Then hail! O King,
>   Whichever you may be,
> To you we sing,
>   But do not bend the knee.
> Then hail! O King.

MARCO *and* GIUSEPPE (*together*).

Come, let's away—our island crown awaits me—
    Conflicting feelings rend my soul apart!
The thought of Royal dignity elates me,
    But leaving thee behind me breaks my heart!
(*Addressing* GIANETTA *and* TESSA)

GIANETTA *and* TESSA (*together*).

Farewell, my love; on board you must be getting;
    But while upon the sea you gaily roam,
Remember that a heart for thee is fretting—
    The tender little heart you've left at home!
GIA.: Now, Marco dear,
    My wishes hear:
        While you're away
    It's understood
    You will be good
        And not too gay.
    To every trace
    Of maiden grace
        You will be blind,
    And will not glance
    By any chance

On womankind!
If you are wise,

You'll shut your eyes
   Till we arrive,
And not address
A lady less
   Than forty-five.
You'll please to frown
On every gown
   That you may see;
And, O my pet,
You won't forget
   You've married me!

And O my darling, O my pet,
Whatever else you may forget,
In yonder isle beyond the sea,
Do not forget you've married me.
TESS.: You'll lay your head
   Upon your bed
      At set of sun.
   You will not sing
   Of anything
      To any one.
   You'll sit and mope
   All day, I hope,
      And shed a tear
   Upon the life
   Your little wife
      Is passing here.
   And if so be

   You think of me,
      Please tell the moon!
   I'll read it all
   In rays that fall
      On the lagoon:
   You'll be so kind

As tell the wind
   How you may be,
And send me words
By little birds
   To comfort me!

And O my darling, O my pet,
Whatever else you may forget,
In yonder isle beyond the sea,
Do not forget you've married me.

QUARTET: O my darling, O my pet, etc.

CHORUS (*during which a 'Xebeque' is hauled alongside the quay*):

Then away　　　{ they / we }　　go to an island fair

That lies in a Southern sea:
We know not where, and we don't much care,
   Wherever that isle may be.

THE MEN (*hauling on boat*): One, two, three,
   Haul!
One, two, three,
   Haul!
One, two, three,
   Haul!
With a will!

ALL: When the breezes are blowing
The ship will be going,

When they don't　　{ we shall / they will }　　all stand still!

Then away　　　{ they / we }　　go to an island fair

We know not where, and we don't much care;
Wherever that isle may be.

SOLO—MARCO.

Away we go
   To a balmy isle,
Where the roses blow
   All the winter while.

ALL (*hoisting sail*): Then away { they / we } go to an island fair
That lies in a Southern sea:

Then away { they / we } go to an island fair

(*The men embark on the 'Xebeque'.* MARCO *and* GIUSEPPE *embracing* GIANETTA *and* TESSA. *The girls wave a farewell to the men as the curtain falls*)

END OF ACT I

Act II

Scene.—*Pavilion in the Court of Barataria.* Marco *and* Giuseppe, *magnificently dressed, are seated on two thrones, occupied in cleaning the crown and the sceptre. The Gondoliers are discovered, dressed, some as courtiers, officers of rank, etc., and others as private soldiers and servants of various degrees. All are enjoying. themselves without reference to social distinctions—some playing cards, others throwing dice, some reading, others playing cup and ball, 'morra', etc.*

Chorus of Men *with* Marco *and* Giuseppe.

Of happiness the very pith
    In Barataria you may see:
A monarchy that's tempered with
    Republican Equality.
This form of government we find
The beau-ideal of its kind—
A despotism strict, combined
    With absolute equality!

Marco *and* Giuseppe.

Two kings, of undue pride bereft,
    Who act in perfect unity,
Whom you can order right-and left
    With absolute impunity.
Who put their subjects at their ease
By doing all they can to please!
And thus, to earn their bread-and-cheese,
    Seize every opportunity.

Chorus: Of happiness the very pith, etc.

Mar.: Gentlemen, we are much obliged to you for your expressions of satisfaction and good feeling—I say, we are much obliged to you for your expressions of satisfaction and good feeling.

All: We heard you.

Mar.: We are delighted, at any time, to fall in with sentiments so charmingly expressed.

ALL: That's all right.

GIU.: At the same time there is just one little grievance that we should like to ventilate.

ALL (*angrily*): What?

GIU.: Don't be alarmed—it's not serious. It is arranged that, until it is decided which of us two is the actual King, we are to act as one person.

GIORGIO: Exactly.

GIU.: Now, although we act as one person, we are, in point of fact, two persons.

ANNIBALE: Ah, I don't think we can go into that. It is a legal fiction, and legal fictions are solemn things. Situated as we are, we can't recognize two independent responsibilities.

GIU.: No; but you can recognize two independent appetites. It's all very well to say we act as one person, but when you supply us with only one ration between us, I should describe it as a legal fiction carried a little too far.

ANNI.: It's rather a nice point. I don't like to express an opinion off-hand. Suppose we reserve it for argument before the full Court?

MAR.: Yes, but what are we to do in the meantime?

MAR. and GIU.: We want our tea.

ANNI.: I think we may make an interim order for double rations on their Majesties entering into the usual undertaking to indemnify in the event of an adverse decision?

GIOR.: That, I think, will meet the case. But you must work hard—stick to it—nothing like work.

GIU.: Oh, certainly. We quite understand that a man who holds the magnificent position of King should do something to justify it. We are called 'Your Majesty', we are allowed to buy ourselves magnificent clothes, our subjects frequently nod to us in the streets, the sentries always return our salutes, and we enjoy the inestimable privilege of heading the subscription lists to all the principal charities. In return for these advantages the least we can do is to make ourselves useful about the Palace.

SONG—GIUSEPPE *with* CHORUS.

Rising early in the morning,
    We proceed to fight the fire,
Then our Majesty adorning

In its workaday attire,
    We embark without delay
    On the duties of the day.

First, we polish off some batches
Of political despatches,
    And foreign politicians circumvent;
Then, if business isn't heavy,
We may hold a Royal *leveé*,
    Or ratify some Acts of Parliament.
Then we probably review the household troops—
With the usual 'Shalloo humps!' and 'Shalloo hoops!'
Or receive with ceremonial and state
An interesting Eastern potentate.
    After that we generally
    Go and dress our private *valet*—
(It's a rather nervous duty—he's a touchy little man)—
    Write some letters literary
    For our private secretary—
He is shaky in his spelling, so we help him if we can.
    Then, in view of cravings inner,
    We, go down and order dinner;
Then we polish the Regalia and the Coronation Plate—
    Spend an hour in titivating
    All our Gentlemen-in-Waiting;
Or we run on little errands for the Ministers of State.
    Oh, philosophers may sing
    Of the troubles of a King;
Yet the duties are delightful, and the privileges great;
    But the privilege and pleasure
    That we treasure beyond measure
Is to run on little errands for the Ministers of State.
CHORUS: Oh, philosophers may sing, etc.
    After luncheon (making merry
    On a bun and glass of sherry),
    If we've nothing in particular to do,
We may make a Proclamation,
Or receive a deputation
    Then we possibly create a Peer or two.

Then we help a fellow-creature on his path
With the Garter or the Thistle or the Bath,
Or we dress and toddle off in semi-state
To a festival, a function, or a *fête*.
 Then we go and stand as sentry
 At the Palace (private entry),
Marching hither, marching, thither, up and down and to and fro,
 While the warrior on duty
 Goes in search of beer and beauty
(And it generally happens that he hasn't far to go).
 He relieves us, if he's able,
 Just in time to lay the table,
Then we dine and serve the coffee, and at half-past twelve or one,
 With a pleasure that's emphatic,
 We retire to our attic,
With the gratifying feeling that our duty has been done!
 Oh, philosophers may sing
 Of the troubles of a King,
But of pleasures there are many and of worries there are none;
 And the culminating pleasure
 That we treasure beyond measure
Is the gratifying feeling that our duty has been done!

CHORUS: Oh, philosophers may sing, etc.

(*Exeunt all but* MARCO *and* GIUSEPPE)

GIU.: Yes, it really is a very pleasant existence. They're all so singularly kind and considerate. You don't find them wanting to do this, or wanting to do that, or saying 'It's my turn now'. No, they let us have all the fun to ourselves, and never seem to grudge it.

MAR.: It makes one feel quite selfish. It almost seems like taking advantage of their good nature.

GIU.: How nice they were about the double rations.

MAR.: Most considerate. Ah! there's only one thing wanting to make us thoroughly comfortable.

GIU.: And that is?

MAR.: The dear little wives we left behind us three months ago.

GIU.: Yes, it is dull without female society. We can do without everything else, but we can't do without that.

MAR.: And if we have that in perfection, we have everything. There is only one recipe for perfect happiness.

SONG—MARCO.

Take a pair of sparkling eyes,
　　Hidden, ever and anon,
　　　　In a merciful eclipse—
　　Do not heed their mild surprise
　　　　Having passed the Rubicon,
　　　　Take a pair of rosy lips;
Take a figure trimly planned—
　　Such as admiration whets—
　　　　(Be particular in this);
Take a tender little hand,
　　Fringed with dainty fingerettes,
　　　　Press it—in parenthesis;—
Ah! Take all these, you lucky man—

Take and keep them, if you can!
Take a pretty little cot—
　　Quite a miniature affair—
　　Hung about with trellised vine,
Furnish it upon the spot
　　With the treasures rich and rare
　　　　I've endeavoured to define.
Live to love and love to live—
　　You will ripen at your ease,
　　　　Growing on the sunny side—
Fate has nothing more to give.
　　You're a dainty man to please
　　　　If you are not satisfied.
Ah! Take my counsel, happy man;
　　Act upon it, if you can!

(*Enter Chorus of Contadine, running in, led by* FIAMETTA *and* VITTORIA.
They are met by all the Ex-Gondoliers, who welcome them heartily)

SCENA—CHORUS OF GIRLS, QUARTET, DUET *and* CHORUS.

Here we are, at the risk of our lives,
From ever so far, and we've brought your wives—

And to that end we've crossed the main,
And don't intend to return again!

FIA.: Though obedience is strong,
  Curiosity's stronger
We waited for long,
  Till we couldn't wait longer.

VIT.: It's imprudent, we know,
  But without your society
Existence was slow,
  And we wanted variety—

BOTH: Existence was slow, and we wanted variety.

ALL: So here we are, at the risk of our lives,
  And we've brought your wives—
  And to that end we've crossed the main,
  And we don't intend to return again!

(*Enter* GIANETTA *and* TESSA. *They rush to the arms of* MARCO *and* GIUSEPPE)

GIU.: Tessa!
TESS.: Giuseppe!
GIA.: Marco!
MAR.: Gianetta!
  } (Embrace)

TESSA *and* GIANETTA.

TESS.: After sailing to this island—
GIA.: Tossing in a manner frightful,
TESS.: We are all once more on dry land—
GIA.: And we find the change delightful,
TESS.: As at home we've been remaining—
  We've not seen you both for ages,
GIA.: Tell me, are you fond of reigning?
  How's the food, and what's the wages?
TESS.: Does your new employment please ye?—
GIA.: How does Royalizing strike you?
TESS.: Is it difficult or easy?—
GIA.: Do you think your subjects like you?
TESS.: I am anxious to elicit,
  Is it plain and easy steering?
GIA.: Take it altogether, is it
  Better fun than gondoliering?

BOTH: We shall both go on requesting
  Till you tell us, never doubt it;
 Everything is interesting,
  Tell us, tell us all about it!

CHORUS: They will both go on requesting, etc.

TESS.: Is. the populace exacting?

GIA.: Do they keep you at a distance?

TESS.: All unaided are you acting,

GIA.: Or do they provide assistance?

TESS.: When you're busy, have you got to
  Get up early in the morning?

GIA.: If you do what you ought not to,
  Do they give the usual warning?

TESS.: With a horse do they equip you?

GIA.: Lots of trumpeting and drumming?

TESS.: Do the Royal tradesmen tip you?

GIA.: Ain't the livery becoming!

TESS.: Does your human being inner
  Feed on everything that nice is?

GIA.: Do they give you wine for dinner;
  Peaches, sugar-plums, and ices?

BOTH: We shall both go on requesting
  Till you tell us, never doubt it;
 Everything is interesting,
  Tell us, tell us all about it!

CHORUS: They will both go on requesting, etc.

MAR.: This is indeed a most delightful surprise!

TESS.: Yes, we thought you'd like it. You see, it was like this. After you left we felt very dull and mopey, and the days crawled by, and you never wrote; so at last I said to Gianetta, 'I can't stand this any longer, those two poor Monarchs haven't got any one to mend their stockings or sew on their buttons or patch their clothes—at least, I hope they haven't—let us all pack up a change and go and see how they're getting on.' And she said, 'Done', and they all said, 'Done'; and we asked old Giacopo to lend us his boat, and he said, 'Done'; and we've crossed the sea, and, thank goodness, *that's* done; and here we are, and—and—*I've* done!

GIA.: And now—which of you is King?

TESS.: And which of us is Queen?

GIU.: That we shan't know until Nurse turns up. But never mind that—the question is, how shall we celebrate the commencement of our honeymoon? Gentlemen, will you allow us to offer you a magnificent banquet?

ALL: We will!

GIU.: Thanks very much; and, ladies, what do you say to a dance?

TESS.: A banquet *and* a dance! Oh, it's too much happiness!

CHORUS *and* DANCE.

Dance a cachucha, fandango, bolero,
Xeres we'll drink—Manzanilla, Montero—
Wine, when it runs in abundance, enhances
The reckless delight of that wildest of dances!
    To the pretty pitter-pitter-patter,
    And the clitter-clitter-clitter-clatter—
        Clitter—clitter—clatter,
        Pitter—pitter—patter,
    Patter, patter, patter, patter, we'll dance.
Old Xeres we'll drink—Manzanilla, Montero;
For wine, when it runs in abundance, enhances
The reckless delight of that wildest of dances!

CACHUCHA.

(*The dance is interrupted by the unexpected appearance of* DON ALHAMBRA, *who looks on with astonishment.* MARCO *and* GIUSEPPE *appear embarrassed. The others run off, except Drummer Boy, who is driven off by* DON ALHAMBRA)

DON AL.: Good evening. Fancy ball?

GIU.: No, not exactly. A little friendly dance. That's all. Sorry you're late.

DON AL.: But I saw a groom dancing, and a footman!

MAR.: Yes. That's the Lord High Footman.

DON AL.: And, dear me, a common little drummer boy!

GIU.: Oh no! That's the Lord High Drummer Boy.

DON AL.: But surely, surely the servants'-hall is the place for these gentry?

GIU.: Oh dear no! We have appropriated the servants'-hall. It's the Royal Apartment, and accessible, only by tickets obtainable at the Lord Chamberlain's office.

MAR.: We really must have some place that we can call our own.

DON AL. (*puzzled*): I'm afraid I'm not quite equal to the intellectual pressure of the conversation.

GIU.: You see, the Monarchy has been re-modelled on Republican principles.

DON AL.: What!

GIU.: All departments rank equally, and everybody is at the head of his department.

DON AL.: I see.

MAR.: I'm afraid you're annoyed.

DON AL.: No. I won't say that. It's not quite what I expected.

GIU.: I'm awfully sorry.

MAR.: So am I.

GIU.: By the by, can I offer you anything after your voyage? A plate of macaroni and a rusk?

DON AL. (*preoccupied*): No, no—nothing—nothing.

GIU.: Obliged to be careful?

DON AL.: Yes—gout. You see, in every Court there are distinctions that must be observed.

GIU. (*puzzled*): There are, are there?

DON AL.: Why, of course. For instance, you wouldn't have a Lord High Chancellor play leapfrog with his own cook.

MAR.: Why not?

DON AL.: Why not! Because a Lord High Chancellor is a personage of great dignity, who should never, under any circumstances, place himself in the position of being told to tuck in his tuppenny, except by noblemen of his own rank. A Lord High Archbishop, for instance, might tell a Lord High Chancellor to tuck in his tuppenny, but certainly not a cook, gentlemen, certainly not a cook.

GIU.: Not even a Lord High Cook?

DON AL.: My good friend, that is a rank that is not recognized at the Lord Chamberlain's office. No, no, it won't do. I'll give you an instance in which the experiment was tried.

SONG—DON ALHAMBRA, *with* MARCO *and* GIUSEPPE.

DON AL.: There lived a King, as I've been told,
In the wonder-working days of old,

When hearts were twice as good as gold,
    And twenty times as mellow.
Good-temper triumphed in his face,
And in his heart he found a place
For all the erring human race
    And every wretched fellow.
When he had Rhenish wine to drink
It made him, very sad to think
That some, at junket or at jink,
    Must be content with toddy.

MAR. and GIU.: With toddy, must be content with toddy.

DON AL.: He wished all men as rich as he
(And he was rich as rich could be),
So to the top of every tree
    Promoted everybody.

MAR. and GIU.: Now, that's the kind of King for me.
He wished all men as rich as he,
So to the top of every tree
    Promoted everybody!

DON AL.: Lord Chancellors were cheap as sprats,
And Bishops in their shovel hats
Were plentiful as tabby cats—
    In point of fact, too many.
Ambassadors cropped up like hay,
Prime Ministers and such as they
Grew like asparagus in May,
    And Dukes were three a penny.
On every side Field-Marshals gleamed,
Small beer were Lords-Lieutenant deemed,
With Admirals the ocean teemed
    All round his wide dominions.

MAR. and GIU.: With Admirals all round his wide dominions.

DON AL.: And Party Leaders you might meet
In twos and threes in every street
Maintaining, with no little heat,
    Their various opinions.

MAR. and GIU.: Now that's a sight you couldn't beat—
Two Party Leaders in each street
Maintaining, with no little heat,

Their various opinions.

DON AL.: That King, although no one denies
　　His heart was of abnormal size,
　　Yet he'd have acted otherwise
　　　If he had been acuter.
　　The end is easily foretold,
　　When every blessed thing you hold
　　Is made of silver, or of gold,
　　　You long for simple pewter.
　　When you have nothing else to wear
　　But cloth of gold and satins rare,
　　For cloth of gold you cease to care—
　　　Up goes the price of shoddy.

MAR. and GIU.: Of shoddy, up goes the price of shoddy.

DON AL.: In short, whoever you may be,
　　To this conclusion you'll agree,
　　When every one is somebodee,
　　　Then no one's anybody!

MAR. and GIU.: Now that's as plain as plain can be,
　　To this conclusion we agree—

ALL: When every one is somebodee,
　　Then no one's anybody!

(GIANETTA *and* TESSA *enter unobserved. The two girls, impelled by curiosity remain listening at the back of the stage*)

DON AL.: And now I have some important news to communicate. His Grace the Duke of Plaza-Toro, Her Grace the Duchess, and their beautiful daughter Casilda—I say their beautiful daughter Casilda—

GIU.: We heard you.

DON AL.: Have arrived at Barataria, and maybe here at any moment.

MAR.: The Duke and Duchess are nothing to us.

DON AL.: But the daughter—the beautiful daughter! Aha! Oh, you're a lucky dog one of you!

GIU.: I think you're a very incomprehensible old gentleman.

DON AL.: Not a bit—I'll explain. Many years ago when you (whichever you are) were a baby, you (whichever you are) were married to a little girl who has grown up to be the most beautiful young lady in Spain. That beautiful young lady will be here to claim you (whichever you are) in half an hour, and I congratulate that one (whichever it is) with all my heart.

Mar.: Married when a baby!

Giu.: But we were married three months ago!

Don Al.: One of you—only one. The other (whichever it is) is an unintentional bigamist.

Gia. and Tess. (*coming forward*): Well, upon my word!

Don Al.: Eh? Who are these young people?

Tess.: Who are we? Why, their wives, of course. We've just arrived.

Don Al.: Their wives! Oh dear, this is very unfortunate! Oh dear, this complicates matters! Dear, dear, what will Her Majesty say?

Gia.: And do you mean to say that one of these Monarchs was already married?

Tess.: And that neither of us will be a Queen?

Don Al.: That is the idea I intended to convey. (Tessa *and* Gianetta *begin to cry*)

Giu. (*to* Tessa): Tessa, my dear, dear child—

Tess.: Get away! perhaps it's you!

Mar. (*to* Gia.): My poor, poor little woman!

Gia.: Don't! Who knows whose husband you are?

Tess.: And pray, why didn't you tell us all about it before. they left Venice?

Don Al.: Because, if I had, no earthly temptation would have induced these gentlemen to leave two such extremely fascinating and utterly irresistible little ladies!

Tess.: There's something in that.

Don Al.: I may mention that you will not be kept long in suspense, as the old lady who nursed the Royal child is at present in the torture chamber, waiting for me to interview her.

Giu.: Poor old girl. Hadn't you better go and put her out of her suspense?

Don Al.: Oh no—there's no hurry—she's s all right. She has all the illustrated papers. However, I'll go and interrogate her, and, in the meantime, may I suggest the absolute propriety of your regarding yourselves as single young ladies. Good evening! (*Exit* Don Alhambra)

Gia.: Well, here's a pleasant state of things!

Mar.: Delightful. One of us is married to two young ladies, and nobody knows which; and the other is married to one young lady whom nobody can identify!

GIA.: And one of us is married to one of you, and the other is married to nobody.

TESS.: But which of you is married to which of us, and what's to become of the other? (*About to cry*)

GIU.: It's quite simple. Observe. Two husbands have managed to acquire three wives. Three wives—two husbands. (*Reckoning up*) That's two-thirds of a husband to each wife.

TESS.: O Mount Vesuvius, here we are in arithmetic! My good Sir, one can't marry a vulgar fraction!

GIU.: You've no right to call me a vulgar fraction.

MAR.: We are getting rather mixed. The situation is entangled. Let's try and comb it out.

QUARTET—MARCO, GIUSEPPE, GIANETTA, TESSA.

In a contemplative fashion,
    And a tranquil frame of mind,
Free from every kind of passion,
    Some solution let us find.
Let us grasp the situation,
    Solve the complicated plot—
Quiet, calm deliberation
    Disentangles every knot.

TESS.: I, no doubt, Giuseppe wedded—   THE OTHERS: In a
    That's, of course, a slice of luck.   contemplative fashion, etc.
He is rather dunder-headed,
    Still distinctly, he's a duck.

GIA.: I, a victim, too, of Cupid,   THE OTHERS: Let us
    Marco married—that is clear.   grasp the situation, etc.
He's particularly stupid,
    Still distinctly, he's a dear.

MAR.: To Gianetta I was mated;   THE OTHERS: Ina-
    I can prove it in a trice: contemplative fashion, etc.
Though her charms are overrated,
    Still I own she's rather nice.

GIU.: I to Tessa, willy-nilly,   THE OTHERS: Let us
    All at once a victim fell.   grasp the situation, etc.
She is what is called a silly,
    Still she answers pretty well.

MAR.: Now when we were pretty babies
      Some one married us, that's clear—
GIA.: And if I can catch her
        I'll pinch her and scratch her
        And send her away with a flea in her ear.
GIU.: He whom that young lady married,
      To receive her can't refuse.
TESS.: If I overtake her
        I'll warrant I'll make her
        To shake in her aristocratical shoes!
GIA. (*to* TESS.): If she married your Giuseppe
        You and he will have to part—
TESS. (*to* GIA.): If I have to do it
        I'll warrant she'll rue it
        I'll teach her to marry the man of my heart!
TESS. (*to* GIA.): If she married Messer Marco
        You're a spinster, that is plain—
GIA. (*to* TESS.): No matter—no matter.
        If I can get at her
        I doubt if her-mother will know her again!
ALL: Quiet, calm deliberation
      Disentangles every knot!

(*Exeunt, pondering*)

(MARCH. *Enter procession of Retainers, heralding approach of* DUKE, DUCHESS, *and* CASILDA. *All three are now dressed with the, utmost magnificence*)

CHORUS OF MEN, *with* DUKE: *and* DUCHESS.

With ducal pomp and ducal pride
    (Announce these comers,
    O ye kettle-drummers!)
Comes Barataria's high-born bride.
    (Ye sounding cymbals clang!)
She comes to claim the Royal hand—
    (Proclaim their Graces,
    O ye double basses!)
Of the King who rules this goodly land.
    (Ye brazen brasses bang!)

DUKE *and* DUCH.: This polite attention touches
    Heart of Duke and heart of Duchess
        Who resign their pet
        With profound regret.
    She of beauty was a model
    When a tiny tiddle-toddle,
        And at twenty-one
        She's excelled by none!

CHORUS: With ducal pomp and ducal pride, etc.

DUKE (*to his attendants*): Be good enough to inform His Majesty that His Grace the Duke of Plaza-Toro, Limited, has arrived, and begs—

CAS.: Desires—

DUCH.: Demands—

DUKE: And demands an audience. (*Exeunt attendants*) And now, my child, prepare to receive the husband to whom you were united under such interesting and romantic circumstances.

CAS.: But which is it? There are two of them!

DUKE: It is true that at present His Majesty is a double gentleman; but as soon as the circumstances of his marriage are ascertained, he will, *ipso facto*, boil down to a single gentleman—thus presenting a unique example of an individual who becomes a single man and a married man by the same operation.

DUCH (*severely*): I have known instances in which the characteristics of both conditions existed concurrently in the same individual.

DUKE: Ah, he couldn't have been a Plaza-Toro.

DUCH.: Oh! couldn't he, though!

CAS.: Well, whatever happens, I shall, of course, be a dutiful wife, but I can never love my husband.

DUKE: I don't know. It's extraordinary what unprepossessing people one can love if one gives one's mind to it.

DUCH.: I loved your father.

DUKE: My love—that remark is a little hard, I think? Rather cruel, perhaps? Somewhat uncalled-for, I venture to believe?

DUCH.: It was very difficult, my dear; but I said to myself, 'That man is a Duke, and I will love him.' Several of my relations bet me I couldn't, but I did—desperately!

Song—Duchess.

On the day when I was wedded
    To your admirable sire,
I acknowledge that I dreaded
    An explosion of his ire.
I was overcome with panic—
For his temper was volcanic,
    And I didn't dare revolt,
    For I feared a thunderbolt!
I was always very wary,
    For his fury was ecstatic—
His refined vocabulary
    Most unpleasantly emphatic.
        To the thunder
            Of this Tartar
        I knocked under
            Like a martyr;
        When intently
            He was fuming,
        I was gently
            Unassuming—
        When reviling
            Me completely,
        I was smiling
            Very sweetly:
Giving him the very best, and getting back the very worst—
That is how I tried to tame your great progenitor—at first!
    But I found that a reliance
        On my threatening appearance,
    And a resolute defiance
        Of marital interference,
    And a gentle intimation
    Of my firm determination
        To see what I could do
        To be wife and husband too
    Was the only thing required
        For to make his temper supple,
    And you couldn't have desired

A more reciprocating couple.
> Ever willing
> > To be wooing,
> We were billing—
> > We were cooing;
> When I merely
> > From him parted,
> We were nearly
> > Broken-hearted—
> When in sequel
> > Reunited,
> We were equal-
> > Ly delighted.

So with double-shotted guns and colours nailed unto the mast,
I tamed your insignificant progenitor—at last!

CAS.: My only hope is that when my husband sees what a shady family he has married into he will repudiate the contract altogether.

DUKE: Shady? A nobleman shady, who is blazing in the lustre of unaccustomed pocket-money? A nobleman shady, who can look back upon ninety-five quarterings? It is not every nobleman who is ninety-five quarters in arrear—I mean, who can look back upon ninety-five of them! And this, just as I have been floated at a premium! Oh fie!

DUCH.: Your Majesty is surely unaware that directly Your Majesty's father came before the public he was applied for over and over again.

DUKE: My dear, Her Majesty's father was in the habit of being applied for over and over again—and very urgently applied for, too—long before he was registered under the Limited Liability Act.

RECITATIVE—DUKE.

To help unhappy commoners, and add to their enjoyment;
Affords a man of noble rank congenial employment;
Of our attempts we offer you examples illustrative:
The work is light, and, I may add, it's most remunerative.

DUET—DUKE *and* DUCHESS.

DUKE: Small titles and orders
For Mayors and Recorders re

I get—and they're highly delighted—
Duch.: They're highly delighted!
Duke: M.P.s baronetted,
  Sham Colonels gazetted,
    And second-rate Aldermen knighted—
Duch.: Yes, Aldermen knighted.
Duke: Foundation-stone laying
  I find very paying:
    It adds a large sum to my makings—
Duch.: Large sums to his makings.
Duke: At charity dinners
  The best of speech-spinners,
    I get ten per cent on the takings—'
Duch.: One-tenth of the takings.
Duch.: I present any lady
  Whose conduct is shady
    Or smacking of doubtful propriety—
Duke: Doubtful propriety.
Duch.: When Virtue would quash her,
  I take and whitewash her,
    And launch her in first-rate society—
Duke: First-rate society!
Duch.: I recommend acres
  Of clumsy dressmakers
    Their fit and their finishing touches—
Duke: Their finishing touches.
Duch.: A sum in addition
  They pay for permission
    To say that they make for the Duchess—
Duke: They make for the Duchess!
Duke: Those pressing prevailers,
  The ready-made tailors,
    Quote me as their great double-barrel—
Duch.: Their great double-barrel—'
Duke: I allow them to do so,
  Though Robinson Crusoe
    Would jib at their wearing apparel—
Duch.: Such wearing apparel!
Duke: I sit, by selection,

Upon the direction
    Of several Companies bubble—
Duch.: All Companies bubble!
Duke: As soon as they're floated
    I'm freely bank-noted—'
        I'm pretty well paid for my trouble—
Duch.: He's paid for his trouble!
Duch.: At middle-class party
    I play at *écarté*—
        And I'm by no means a beginner—'
Duke (*significantly*): She's not a beginner.
Duch.: To one of my station
    The remuneration—
        Five guineas a night and my dinner—
Duke: And wine with her dinner.
Duch.: I write letters blatant
    On medicines patent—
        And use any other you mustn't—
Duke: Believe me, you mustn't—
Duch.: And vow my complexion
    Derives its perfection
    From somebody's soap—which it doesn't—
Duke (*significantly*): It certainly doesn't!
Duke: We're ready as witness
    To any one's fitness
        To fill any place or preferment—
Duch.: A place or preferment.
Duch.: We're often in waiting
    At junket or *fêting*,
        And sometimes attend an interment—
Duke: We enjoy an interment.
Both: In short, if you'd kindle
    The spark of a swindle,
        Lure simpletons into your clutches—
        Yes; into your clutches.
    Or hoodwink a debtor,
    You cannot do better
Duch.: Than trot out a Duke or a Duchess—
Duke: A Duke or a Duchess!

(*Enter* MARCO *and* GIUSEPPE)

DUKE: Ah! Their Majesties. Your Majesty! (*Bows with great ceremony*)

MAR.: The Duke of Plaza-Toro, I believe?

DUKE: The same. (MARCO *and* GIUSEPPE *offer to shake hands with him. The* DUKE *bows ceremoniously. They endeavour to imitate him*) Allow me to

present—

GIU.: The young lady one of us married?

(MARCO *and* GIUSEPPE *offer to shake hands with her.* CASILDA *curtsies formally. They endeavour to imitate her*)

CAS.: Gentlemen, I am the most obedient servant of one of you. (*Aside*) Oh, Luiz!

DUKE: I am now about to address myself to the gentleman whom my daughter married; the other may allow his attention to wander if he likes, for what I am about to say does not concern him. Sir, you will find in this young lady a combination of excellences which you would search for in vain in any young lady who had not the good fortune to be my daughter. There is some little doubt as to which of you is the gentleman I am addressing, and which is the gentleman who is allowing his attention to wander; but when that doubt is solved, I shall say (still addressing the attentive gentleman), 'Take her, and may she make you happier than her mother has made me.'

DUCH.: Sir!

DUKE: If possible. And now there is a little matter to which I think I am entitled to take exception. I come here in state with Her Grace the Duchess and Her Majesty my daughter, and what do I find? Do I find, for instance, a guard of honour to receive me? No!

MAR. and GIU.: No.

DUKE: The town illuminated? No!

MAR. and GIU.: No.

DUKE: Refreshment provided? No!

MAR. and GIU.: No.

DUKE: A Royal salute fired? No!

MAR. and GIU.: No.

DUKE: Triumphal arches erected? No!

MAR. and GIU.: No.

DUKE: The bells set ringing?

MAR. and GIU.: No.

DUKE: Yes—one—the Visitors', and I rang it myself. It is not enough! It is not enough!

GIU.: Upon my honour, I'm very sorry; but you see, I was brought up in a gondola, and my ideas of politeness are confined to taking off my cap to my passengers when they tip me.

DUCH.: That's all very well in its way, but it is not enough.

GIU.: I'll take off anything else in reason.

DUKE: But a Royal Salute to my daughter—it costs so little.

CAS.: Papa, I don't want a salute.

GIU.: My dear sir, as soon as we know which of us is entitled to take that liberty she shall have as many salutes as she likes.

MAR.: As for guards of honour and triumphal arches, you don't know our people—they wouldn't stand it.

GIU.: They are very off-hand with us—very off-hand indeed.

DUKE: Oh, but you mustn't allow that—you must keep them in proper discipline, you must impress your Court with your importance. You want deportment—carriage—

GIU.: We've got a carriage.

DUKE: Manner—dignity. There must be a good deal of this sort of thing—(*business*)—and a little of this sort of thing—(*business*)—and possibly just a *soupçon* of. this sort of thing!—(*business*)—and so on. Oh, it's very useful, and most effective. Just attend to me. You are a King—I am a subject. Very good—

GAVOTTE—DUKE, DUCHESS, CASILDA,
MARCO *and* GIUSEPPE.

DUKE: I am a courtier grave and serious
    Who is about to kiss your hand:
Try to combine a pose imperious
    With a demeanour nobly bland.

MAR. and GIU.: Let us combine a pose imperious
    With a demeanour nobly bland.

(MARCO *and* GIUSEPPE *endeavour to carryout his instructions*)

DUKE: That's, if anything, too unbending—
    Too aggressively stiff and grand;

(*They suddenly modify their attitudes*)

    Now to the other extreme you're tending—
    Don't be so deucedly condescending!

DUCH. and CAS. Now to the other extreme you're tending—
    Don't be so dreadfully condescending!
MAR. and GIU.: Oh, hard to please some noblemen seem!
    At first, if anything, too unbending;
  Off we go to the other extreme
  Too confoundedly condescending!
DUKE: Now a gavotte perform sedately
    Offer your hand with conscious pride;
  Take an attitude not too stately,
    Still sufficiently dignified.
MAR. and GIU.: Now for an attitude not too stately,
    Still sufficiently dignified.
(*They endeavour to carry out his instructions*)
DUKE (*beating time*): Oncely, twicely—oncely, twicely
    Bow impressively ere you glide. (*They do so*)
  Capital both, capital both—you've caught it nicely!
  That is the style of thing precisely!
DUCH and CAS.: Capital-both, capital both—they've caught it nicely!
  That is the style of thing precisely!
MAR. and GIU.: Oh, sweet to earn a nobleman's praise!
    Capital both, capital both—we've caught it nicely!
  Supposing he's right in what he says,
    This is the style of thing precisely!
(GAVOTTE. *At the end exeunt* DUKE: *and* DUCHESS, *leaving* CASILDA
with MARCO *and* GIUSEPPE,)
GIU. (*to* MARCO): The old birds have gone away and left the young
    chickens together. That's called tact.
MAR.: It's very awkward. We really ought to tell her how we are
    situated. It's not fair to the girl.
GIU.: Then why don't you do it?
MAR.: I'd rather not—you.
GIU.: I don't know how to begin. (*To* CASILDA) A—Madam—I—we,
    that is, several of us—
CAS.: Gentlemen, I am bound to listen to you; but it is right to tell
    you that, not knowing I was married in infancy, I am over head
    and ears in love with somebody else.
GIU.: Our case exactly! We are over head and ears in love with
    somebody else! (*Enter* GIANETTA *and* TESSA.) In point of fact,
    with our wives!

CAS.: Your wives! Then you are married?

TESS.: It's not our fault.

GIA.: We knew nothing about it.

BOTH: We are sisters in misfortune.

CAS.: My good girls, I don't blame you. Only before we go any further we must really arrive at some satisfactory arrangement, or we shall get hopelessly complicated.

QUINTET *and* FINALE.—MARCO, GIUSEPPE, CASILDA, GIANETTA, TESSA.

ALL: Here is a case unprecedented!
>Here are a King and Queen ill-starred!
>Ever since marriage was first invented
>Never was known a case so hard!

MAR. and GIU.: I may be said to have been bisected,
>By a profound catastrophe!

CAS., GIA. and TESS.: Through a calamity unexpected
>I am divisible into three!

ALL: O moralists all,
>How can you call
>Marriage a state of unitee,
>When excellent husbands are bisected,
>And wives divisible into three?
>O moralists all,
>How can you call
>Marriage a state of union true?

CAS., GIA. and TESS.: One-third of myself is married to half of ye or you.

MAR. and GIU.: When half of myself has married one-third of ye or you?

(*Enter* DON ALHAMBRA, *followed by* DUKE, DUCHESS, *and all the* CHORUS)

FINALE.

RECITATIVE—DON ALHAMBRA.

Now let the loyal lieges gather round—
The Prince's foster-mother has been found!

She will declare, to silver clarion's sound,
    The rightful King—let him forthwith be crowned!
CHORUS: She will declare, etc.
(DON ALHAMBRA *brings forward* INEZ, *the Prince's foster-mother*)
TESS.: Speak, woman, speak—
DUKE: We're all attention!
GIA.: The news we seek—
DUCH.: This moment mention.
CAS.: To us they bring
DON AL.: His foster-mother:
MAR.: Is he the King?
GIU.: Or this my brother?
ALL: Speak, woman, speak, etc.

RECITATIVE—INEZ.

The Royal Prince was by the King entrusted
To my fond care, ere I grew old and crusted;
When traitors came to steal his son reputed,
My own small boy I deftly substituted!
The villains fell into the trap completely—
I hid the Prince away—still sleeping sweetly:
I called him 'son' with pardonable slyness—
His name, Luiz! Behold his Royal Highness!
(*Sensation.* LUIZ: *ascends the throne, crowned and robed as King*)
CAS. (*rushing to his arms*): Luiz.
LUIZ: Casilda! (*Embrace*)
ALL: Is this indeed the King?
        Oh, wondrous revelation!
    Oh, unexpected thing!
        Unlooked-for situation!
MAR., GIA., GIU. *and* TESS.: This statement we receive
        With sentiments conflicting;
    Our hearts rejoice and grieve,
        Each other contradicting;
    To those whom we adore
        We can be reunited—
    On one point rather sore,
        But, on the whole, delighted!

Luiz: When others claimed thy dainty hand,
    I waited—waited—waited,
Duke: As prudence (so I understand)
    Dictated—tated—tated.
Cas.: By virtue of our early vow
    Recorded—corded—corded,
Duch.: Your pure and patient love is now
    Rewarded—warded—warded.
All: Then hail, O King of a Golden Land,
    And the high-born bride who claims his hand!
    The past is dead, and you gain your own,
    A royal crown and a golden throne!
(*All kneel* Luiz. *crowns* Casilda)
All: Once more *gondolieri*,
    Both skilful and wary,
    Free from this quandary
    Contented are we. Ah!
    From Royalty flying,
    Our gondolas plying,
    And merrily crying
    Our *'premé,' 'stallì'* Ah!
So good-bye, cachucha, fandango, bolero—
    We'll dance a farewell to that measure—
Old Xeres, adieu—Manzanilla—Montero—
    We leave you with feelings of pleasure!

CURTAIN

A Note About the Author

W.S. Gilbert (1836–1911) and Arthur Sullivan (1842–1900) were theatrical collaborators during the nineteenth century. Prior to their partnership, Gilbert wrote and illustrated stories as a child, eventually developing his signature "topsy-turvy" style. Sullivan was raised in a musical family where he learned to play multiple instruments at an early age. Together, their talents would help produce a successful series of comic operas. Some notable titles include *The Pirates of Penzance*, *The Sorcerer*, *H.M.S. Pinafore*, and *The Mikado*.

A Note from the Publisher

Spanning many genres, from non-fiction essays to literature classics to children's books and lyric poetry, Mint Edition books showcase the master works of our time in a modern new package. The text is freshly typeset, is clean and easy to read, and features a new note about the author in each volume. Many books also include exclusive new introductory material. Every book boasts a striking new cover, which makes it as appropriate for collecting as it is for gift giving. Mint Edition books are only printed when a reader orders them, so natural resources are not wasted. We're proud that our books are never manufactured in excess and exist only in the exact quantity they need to be read and enjoyed.

bookfinity™

Discover more of your favorite classics with Bookfinity™.

- Track your reading with custom book lists.
- Get great book recommendations for your personalized Reader Type.
- Add reviews for your favorite books.
- AND MUCH MORE!

Visit **bookfinity.com** and take the fun Reader Type quiz to get started.

Enjoy our classic and modern companion pairings!

Classic & Modern

www.ingramcontent.com/pod-product-compliance
Lightning Source LLC
Chambersburg PA
CBHW020606030426
42337CB00013B/1243